POINTERS

CASTLES & FORTS

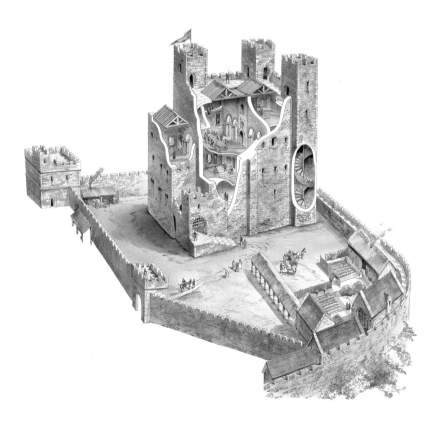

BROWN BEAR BOOKS

Published by Brown Bear Books Ltd
First Floor
9–17 St Albans Place
London N1 0NX

ISBN 978-1-78121-320-9

A catalogue record for this book is available from
the British Library.

Designer: Melissa Roskell
Editor: Dawn Titmus
Design manager: Keith Davis
Editorial director: Lindsey Lowe
Children's publisher: Anne O'Daly
Text: Miriam Moss
Illustrations: Chris Forsey

Printed in China

Contents

Introduction

The best way to avoid attack by enemies is to live somewhere that is difficult to reach. In ancient times, people built their homes on isolated rocky headlands, steep cliff edges and high, flat-topped hills. They gradually added obstacles such as walls to make invading the settlements even more difficult.

The word 'castle' means a building with massive defences. It might be a fortress with thick walls or a large house with battlements. Some castles were magnificent homes, with great dining halls, grand chambers, large kitchens and private chapels. People living in a castle always had to be ready for war. Attackers used powerful catapults to hurl missiles. The castle archers fired crossbows at the enemy through the castle's slit-like windows. If the attackers managed to get inside the castle, people fought with swords, axes and maces. By the 16th century, attackers were using cannon. Castle walls could not stand up to attack by cannon. People stopped building castles for defence.

Many of the ancient castles we visit today seem empty and silent. But when people lived in them, they were noisy, bustling, colourful places, as you will find out.

Bronze Age Citadel

Mycenae is the most famous Bronze Age citadel in Greece. Built on a rocky hilltop, it lies half hidden by deep ravines (narrow valleys) and a rampart. In the 13th century BCE, Mycenae was the citadel of King Agamemnon. His court was famous for its fabulous wealth.

In the 19th century, archaeologists began to excavate (dig up) the royal tombs at Mycenae. They found a hoard of golden treasures, including vases, face masks and swords with golden hilts (handles).

3 The royal tombs were built into the hillside. They were long passages with chambers cut out of the rock at the ends.

Postern Gate

1 The hole in the wall is called a sally port. Surprise attacks could be launched on the enemy through the hole.

2 This stepped tunnel led to a secret water supply. It would have been important when the castle was under siege.

4 The citadel was surrounded by walls 900 metres (2,953 feet) long and 5 metres (16 feet) thick. They may once have been 10–12 m (33–39 feet) high. They were built of massive stones, each weighing 12 tonnes (11.8 tons).

5 The palace was finely decorated. The walls were covered with frescoes. The floors were first covered in plaster, then divided into squares and decorated.

6 The Lion Gate marks the entrance to the citadel. The approach to the gate runs between two bastion walls, so enemies could be attacked before they reached the gate.

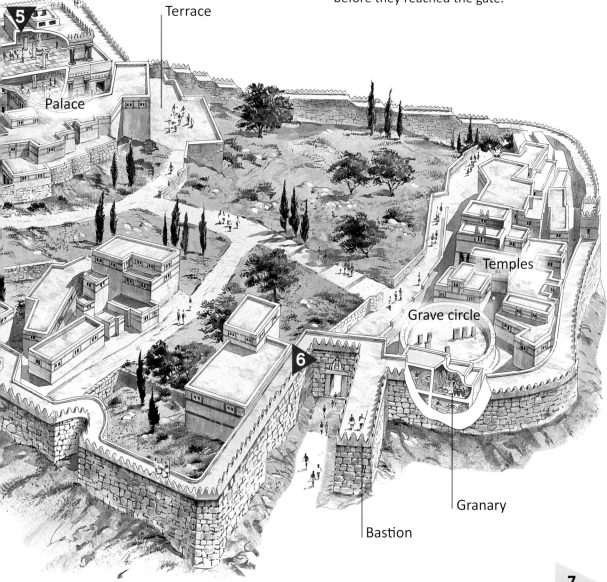

Terrace

Palace

Temples

Grave circle

Granary

Bastion

Iron Age Hill Fort

Cadbury Castle was an Iron Age hill fort in Somerset, England. Romans attacked it in about 60 CE and its Celtic inhabitants were massacred (killed). By around 500 CE, however, Cadbury had become one of the largest, strongest forts in England.

Legend says that it was the site of Camelot – the court of King Arthur and the famous Knights of the Round Table. The last time Cadbury was occupied was by the Saxon king Ethelred II, from 1009 to 1019 CE. He defended it against attack by the Danes.

2 The hill had four or five lines of Iron Age banks and ditches, which attackers found very difficult to get past.

3 After the Roman massacre, the defenders' bodies were left unburied. Brooches have been found inside the gate, as well as more than 100 iron weapons and scattered bones.

1 During the 5th century, the defensive wall around the fort was made of a timber framework with planks or wickerwork on top. Earth and rubble were piled up, and it was finished off with a facing (layer) of dry stonework.

▲ Banked hill

A steep hill became harder for an enemy to climb if defenders dug banks and ditches around the sides. They built a bank, followed by a ditch and then a steep slope. The attackers would have to cross these to reach the castle. As the attackers approached, the defenders could use their weapons on them.

4 The entrance passage was lined with stone and had a single guard chamber above it. Feet, hooves and wheels have worn the rock path into a hollow more than 1.8 m (6 feet) deep.

Rampart

5 The large dining hall had a thatched roof and timber frame, filled with wattle and daub. Part of the hall was separated off as a private chamber.

5

3

6

South-west gate tower

6 This building is one of three, probably military, rectangular buildings that have been excavated at Cadbury.

4

Jewish Fort

Masada stands on an outcrop of rock high above the desert overlooking the Dead Sea in Israel. Herod the Great built the fort. In 73 CE, a group of 960 Jews used Masada as their base while they battled for freedom from Roman rule.

One night, the leader of the Jews persuaded his people to end their own lives rather than be taken prisoner. Each man had to kill his own family. Ten men were chosen to kill the rest, and the last remaining man had to set fire to the palace and then kill himself. When the Romans reached Masada the next day, they were met with a terrible silence.

1 The bath house had a main pool and two small pools. One small pool collected water for the main pool. The other small pool was for bathers to wash their hands and feet before entering the main pool.

2 King Herod the Great built a palace for himself on three levels, with terraces overlooking the Dead Sea.

3 The casemate wall surrounding the fortress had many towers as an additional defence. Inside the wall were 110 rooms.

Snake Path Gate

3

Storehouses

Bath house

1

2

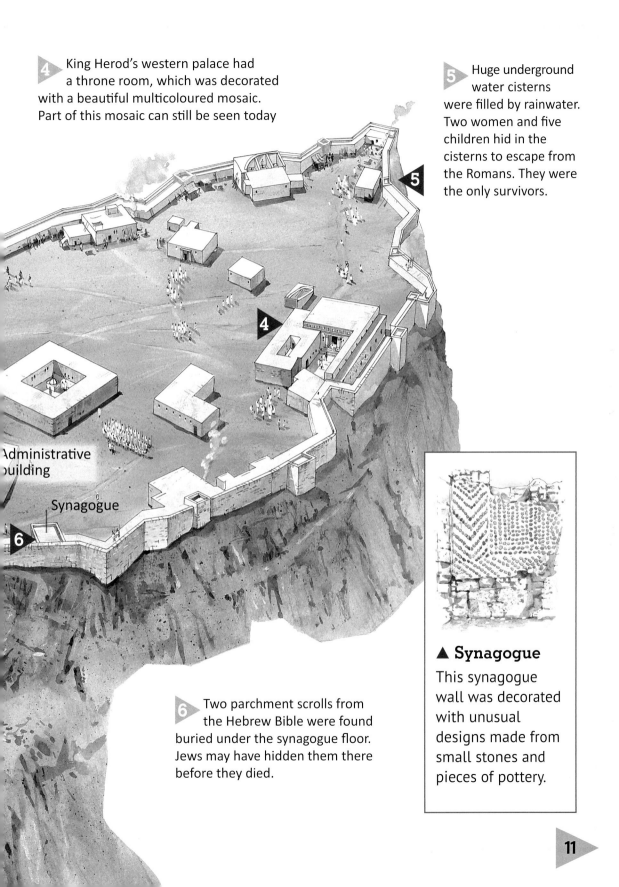

4 King Herod's western palace had a throne room, which was decorated with a beautiful multicoloured mosaic. Part of this mosaic can still be seen today

5 Huge underground water cisterns were filled by rainwater. Two women and five children hid in the cisterns to escape from the Romans. They were the only survivors.

Administrative Building

Synagogue

6 Two parchment scrolls from the Hebrew Bible were found buried under the synagogue floor. Jews may have hidden them there before they died.

▲ Synagogue

This synagogue wall was decorated with unusual designs made from small stones and pieces of pottery.

Norman Keep

The castle at Rochester, England, is a good example of a Norman square keep. During the 11th and 12th centuries, the Normans (people who came from France) occupied England and built many castles. The castle served not only as a fortress, but also as a home for its Norman lord, a court and a prison.

Rochester was one of the first English castles to be fortified with stone instead of timber. In 1215, it was defended against King John for seven weeks, even though the attackers battered it with stone-throwing machines and set fire to the keep.

1 The outer bailey was used for sports contests. It also housed all the people who worked in the castle.

2 The forebuilding protected the entrance. Visitors had to pass through a portcullis, a guard tower and a small lobby.

3 The mural gallery was used by minstrels (musicians). It was also used as an exercise space during bad weather or as an extra sleeping area.

◀ The castle hoarding

The hoarding was a wooden gallery, which was attached to the top of the outer wall of the castle when it was under attack. Timber beams held up the hoarding. Defenders used it as a platform from which they could drop heavy objects on the attackers below.

Battlements

4 The semicircular corner tower was built after the siege in 1215. Its curved wall was designed to deflect (turn) missiles away from the castle walls.

5 The wall walk provided an excellent lookout point. After a siege in 1088, the wooden defences were replaced by stronger walls of stone.

Spiral staircase

6 The keep was not only for military defence. It also provided living quarters for its owners. The keep at Rochester had a basement and three floors above it.

Guard tower

Portcullis

Outer staircase

Inner bailey

Cross wall

Crusader Castle

Krak des Chevaliers, in Syria, was built in 1170 by the Crusaders. They were Christians fighting the Muslims for control of Jerusalem and the Holy Land. The castle was important because it lay in the only mountain pass that could be used all year.

The castle's gigantic towers were made from massive stone blocks. There was a strong keep, with walls 8.5 m (28 feet) thick in places. The Great Hall was used for meetings of the Chapter of the Hospitallers – the Crusader knights who governed Krak. The castle also contained a storeroom that could hold enough food to feed the garrison for five years.

1 A Crusader chapel was built into the rampart. It was converted into a mosque when the Muslims captured Krak.

2 The entrance to the castle had a long passage with guard rooms on either side. These opened onto a hidden moat between the inner and outer walls.

3 The Hall of Massive Pillars stood on one side of the courtyard. It contained kitchens, dining rooms and storerooms.

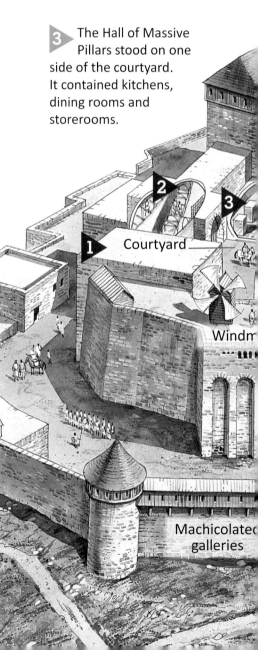

Courtyard

Windm

Lookout tower

Machicolated galleries

4 The Great Hall was 27 m (89 feet) long and 7.5 m (25 feet) wide. It had a high, pointed, arched roof.

5 A square tower jutted out from the outer rampart. It defended the narrow bridge of the aqueduct, which supplied the moat with water.

6 The One Hundred and Twenty Metre Hall contained a well and four bread ovens. It was also used as a warehouse. Lavatories were built into the north wall.

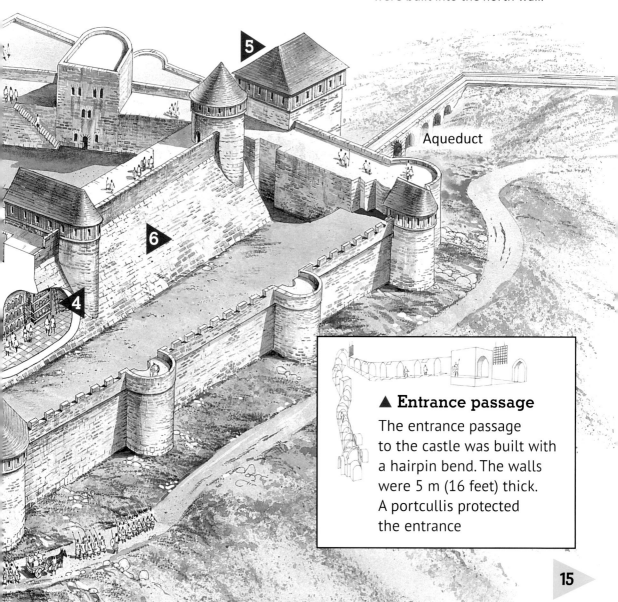

Aqueduct

▲ **Entrance passage**

The entrance passage to the castle was built with a hairpin bend. The walls were 5 m (16 feet) thick. A portcullis protected the entrance

13th-century Castle

Conwy Castle, in North Wales, was built by the English king Edward I. It was one of several new castles built to help him conquer Wales. Edward I was a well-travelled, experienced soldier. He knew that the corners on the old square keeps were blind spots, which meant the enemy could easily undermine them. So he built Conwy Castle in a narrow, rectangular shape, defended by eight strong, round towers.

Conwy was designed in two parts. One part for the king was arranged like a castle within a castle. This part could be defended separately. The other part was for the troop garrison and overlooked the town. The building materials often had to be carried long distances, yet it took just four years to complete Conwy Castle, from 1283 to 1287. In those days, the walls were whitewashed so that the castle stood out as a shining symbol of royal power to all who saw it.

1 The walled town was built at the same time as the castle. The townspeople were protected not only by the wall but also by the castle and its defences.

2 Loopholes were slit-like or cross-shaped openings in the castle wall. Archers inside the wall could fire their arrows through them, safe from attack.

Chapel Tower

Stockhouse Tower

Kitchen Tow

North-west Tow

Drawbridge

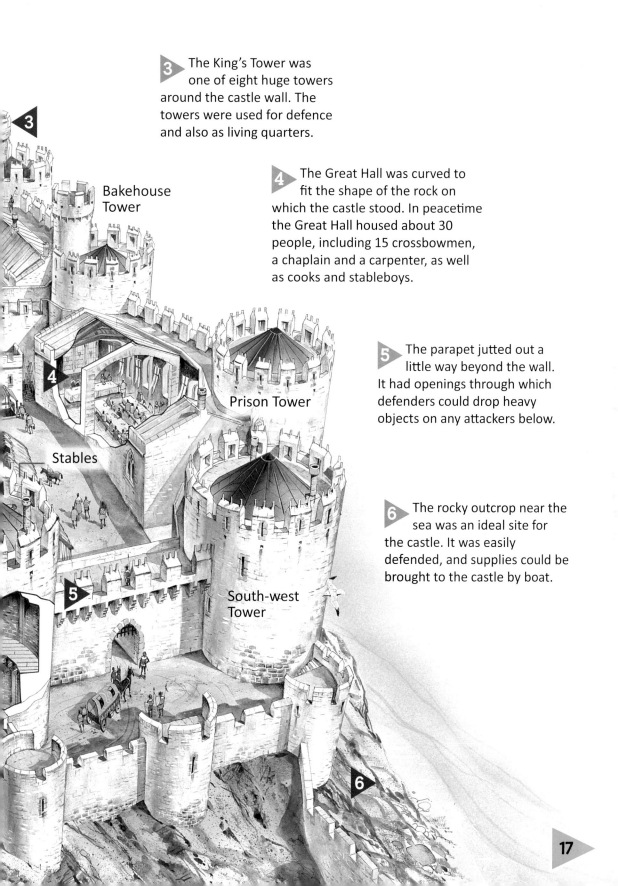

3 The King's Tower was one of eight huge towers around the castle wall. The towers were used for defence and also as living quarters.

4 The Great Hall was curved to fit the shape of the rock on which the castle stood. In peacetime the Great Hall housed about 30 people, including 15 crossbowmen, a chaplain and a carpenter, as well as cooks and stableboys.

5 The parapet jutted out a little way beyond the wall. It had openings through which defenders could drop heavy objects on any attackers below.

6 The rocky outcrop near the sea was an ideal site for the castle. It was easily defended, and supplies could be brought to the castle by boat.

Bakehouse Tower

Prison Tower

Stables

South-west Tower

14th-century Castle

Bodiam Castle was one of the last castles to be built in England. It was the result of centuries of experience in castle design. It is a good example of a castle that was built for defence but that was also a comfortable home.

In the 14th century, the French attacked several of the ports along the south coast of England. As a result, the coastal defences had to be made stronger. In 1385, a rich knight, Sir Edward Dalyngrigge, was given royal permission to fortify his manor house at Bodiam in Sussex. It became Bodiam Castle. People were now using firearms for defence, and Bodiam was one of the first castles to have gunports.

1 There were plenty of rooms for guests in the little chambers in the gatehouses and turrets.

▶ Keyhole gunports

The gatehouse had keyhole gunports. The primitive guns were shaped like tubes and could be placed through the round hole. The gunner could look through the slit above to take aim.

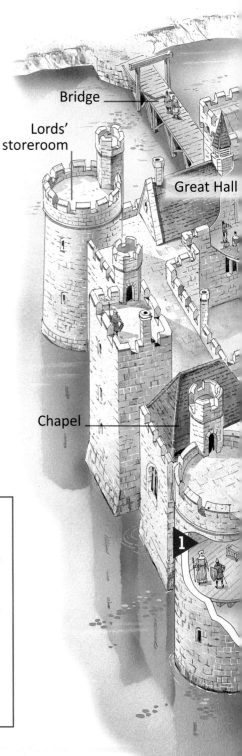

Bridge

Lords' storeroom

Great Hall

Chapel

1

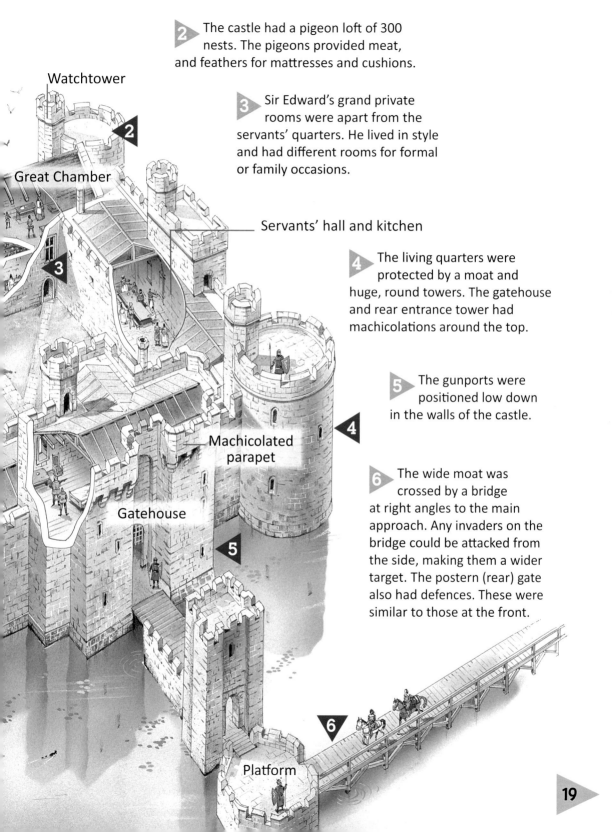

2 The castle had a pigeon loft of 300 nests. The pigeons provided meat, and feathers for mattresses and cushions.

Watchtower

3 Sir Edward's grand private rooms were apart from the servants' quarters. He lived in style and had different rooms for formal or family occasions.

Great Chamber

Servants' hall and kitchen

4 The living quarters were protected by a moat and huge, round towers. The gatehouse and rear entrance tower had machicolations around the top.

5 The gunports were positioned low down in the walls of the castle.

Machicolated parapet

6 The wide moat was crossed by a bridge at right angles to the main approach. Any invaders on the bridge could be attacked from the side, making them a wider target. The postern (rear) gate also had defences. These were similar to those at the front.

Gatehouse

Platform

French Château

In the 16th century, François I, the King of France, decided to built a splendid new castle, or château, on the bank of the River Loire at Chambord, France. A hunting lodge had originally stood on the site. The château of Chambord was designed by the Italian architect Domenico da Cortona. It was a huge project. Some 1,800 men worked under three master masons.

Chambord was designed like a fortified castle. The massive keep, corner towers, moat and cannon openings in the battlements are all features that are more usually found in a castle.

2 ▶ The castle was built with a wide moat. People entered the castle by crossing a bridge facing the keep.

1 ▶ Chambord has an elaborate skyline of towers and turrets. They are an unusual mixture of French and Italian architectural styles.

3 The château was begun in 1519. It took many years to complete. The final detail, the gilded lead roof of the keep, was completed in 1546.

▶ **Master masons**

Three master masons worked on the project. They are thought to have changed the architect's original plans. They created the extraordinary mixture of plain and decorative styles found at Chambord.

4 In the centre of the castle there is a huge double spiral staircase. Two people could climb up it without ever meeting each other.

5 The terrace has projecting stones, called corbels. These were designed for cannons, although they were never used for that purpose.

6 The château has 400 rooms – private chambers for King François and his family, guest rooms, audience chambers, dining rooms and kitchens.

Japanese Castle

Between 1568 and 1600, powerful military warlords built many castles in Japan. The grand architecture and rich interiors of the castles were signs of the status and authority of the warlords, who constantly battled with each other.

The finest surviving castle of this period is Himeji-jo (*jo* means 'castle' in Japanese). The original building dated from the 14th century. It was enlarged by Hideyoshi, a military leader and master of siege warfare, who owned it from 1577. Another important military leader, Ikeda Terumasa, gave Himeji-jo its present majestic appearance in about 1600.

Gable

1 Craftspeople in workshops made gold lacquer bowls and trays for use at banquets, and fine tea bowls for tea ceremonies.

2 Japanese castles had massive walls made of rocks fitted together without mortar. Sometimes timber was used in their construction.

3 The central compound contained the donjon (keep). Japanese castles were unusual in having decorated gables (sloping ends of a pitched roof). Three smaller donjons were clustered around the main building.

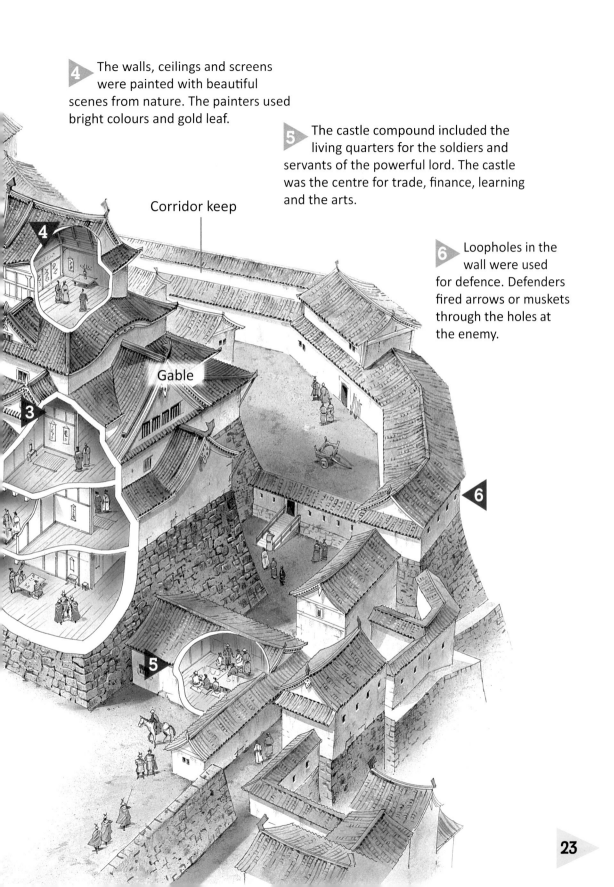

4 The walls, ceilings and screens were painted with beautiful scenes from nature. The painters used bright colours and gold leaf.

5 The castle compound included the living quarters for the soldiers and servants of the powerful lord. The castle was the centre for trade, finance, learning and the arts.

Corridor keep

6 Loopholes in the wall were used for defence. Defenders fired arrows or muskets through the holes at the enemy.

Gable

Indian Fortress

In 1628, Shah Jahan became Emperor of India. He decided to move his capital from Agra to Delhi. In 1638, he began planning his new city. Inside the city he built a great fortified citadel containing a royal palace. It was called the Red Fort, after the deep red colour of its 30-m (98-foot) high sandstone walls.

1 The Diwan-i-Am (Hall of Public Audience) is made up of many arches. The red sandstone used for these buildings was covered by a fine white plaster, which was polished to look like marble.

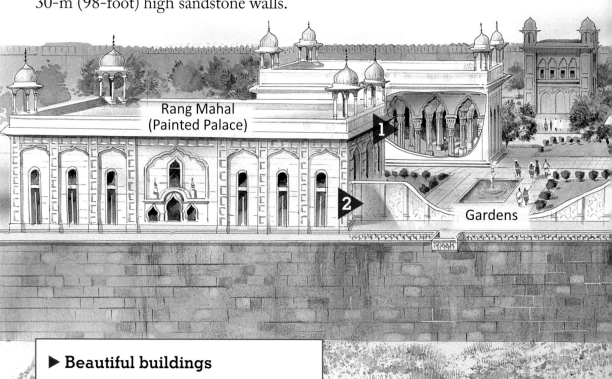

Rang Mahal (Painted Palace)

Gardens

▶ Beautiful buildings

The emperor's architects were famous for their beautiful buildings. Inside the palace enclosure were decorated pavilions, marble palaces, courtyards and galleries with carved archways, marble floors and high, domed ceilings. Many were decorated with gold and silver and precious stones.

2 Balustrades and screens of marble, which looked like fine lace, protected the beautiful gardens. A canal called the Canal of Paradise supplied water for the fountains and pools.

3 Each morning, the emperor inspected newly captured elephants. The elephants were scrubbed clean and painted black, then covered with embroidered cloth and silver bells.

5 The famous Peacock Throne stood in the Diwan-i-Khas on a huge marble slab. The throne was covered by a gold canopy on pillars sparkling with emeralds.

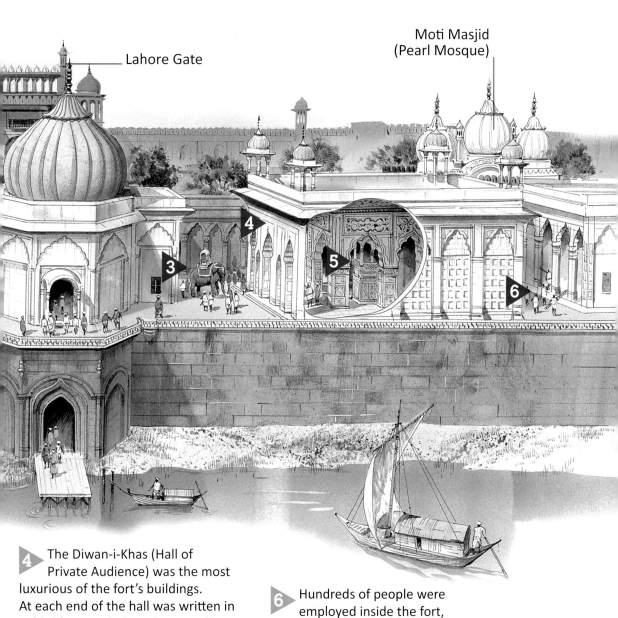

Lahore Gate

Moti Masjid (Pearl Mosque)

4 The Diwan-i-Khas (Hall of Private Audience) was the most luxurious of the fort's buildings. At each end of the hall was written in gold: 'If on earth there is a paradise, then this is it, yes this is it, this is it.'

6 Hundreds of people were employed inside the fort, including bakers, torch makers, perfume makers and goldsmiths.

American Civil War Fort

I n the 19th century, a dispute about slavery led to the southern states of the United States of America leaving the Union of States and becoming the Confederate States of America. The northern states remained in the Union of States.

Fort Sumter in South Carolina faced a difficult choice. It was a Union fort in the middle of Confederate territory. The small garrison of 10 officers and 73 men was under the command of Major Robert Anderson. In 1861, the governor of South Carolina ordered Major Anderson to surrender. He refused and thousands of Confederate troops surrounded the fort. They bombarded the fort with mortar shells and the fort was set ablaze. The American Civil War had begun.

2 Only two lives were lost at Fort Sumter. Both men died after the final surrender. When Major Anderson fired his last salute, a charge of gunpowder exploded, killing one gunner instantly and fatally wounding another.

Buildin materi

2

Stair Tower

1 Fort Sumter was a five-sided stronghold made from brick. It stood on an island in Charleston Harbor, South Carolina.

3 The fort was designed for a garrison of 650 men. There was space for 135 guns, arranged in tiers (levels) around the walls of the fort. The middle tier was never finished, and guns were placed only on the top and bottom tiers.

4 In 1865, the Confederate troops abandoned the fort. The (now) Major General Anderson returned on the anniversary of his departure to raise the same Union flag that he had lowered four years before.

5 The position of the fort on an island at the mouth of the harbour meant it could defend a wide range of territory, both on land and at sea.

Soldiers' barracks

Officers' quarters

Sand

Lantern

6 The walls of the fort were 1.5 to 3 m (5 to 10 feet) thick and rose 12 m (39 feet) above the water.

Fairy-tale Castle

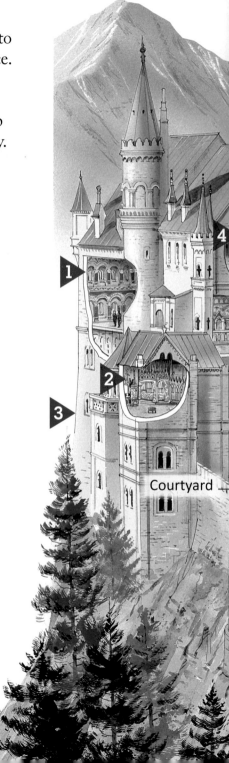

Courtyard

By the 19th century, people stopped building castles for defence. But rich people continued to build them to show off their wealth and importance.

King Ludwig II started building his fairy-tale castle, Neuschwanstein, in 1869. It stands high up in the mountains of Bavaria in southern Germany. Ludwig became king when he was only 18 years old. He was shy and felt misunderstood by the world around him. He decided to shut himself away and surround himself with beautiful things. Instead of an architect, he hired a theatre set designer to built Neuschwanstein.

1 Ludwig had six paintings of saintly past kings hung in his throne room. They were meant to show his belief in the religious connection between kings and God.

2 In the king's bedroom on 12 June 1886, Ludwig's enemies declared him insane. Ludwig died mysteriously the next day. He and his doctor had gone for a walk and were found dead in a lake.

3 Huge amounts of materials were needed to build the castle. People pulled them up the mountain using a steam-operated crane. In one year, 472 tonnes (465 tons) of marble, 1,581 tonnes (1,556 tons) of sandstone and 400,000 bricks were used.

4 The name 'Neuschwanstein' means 'new swan stone'. There was a swan in one form or another in almost every room in the castle. The swan was a symbol of purity and it was King Ludwig's favourite creature.

5 The king had a grotto full of stalactites built between the living room and the study. The stalactites were made of plaster of Paris.

5

ingers' Hall

Spiral staircase

6 The castle employed hundreds of people from the villages around it. It took them almost 20 years to complete the building.

6

Gatehouse

Glossary

Words in SMALL CAPITALS indicate cross-references.

aqueduct A bridge that carries water.

archaeologist A person who studies the remains left by people in the past.

bailey The outer court of a castle, which could be defended from attack. There was sometimes an outer bailey and an inner bailey.

balustrade An ornamental rail.

barbican An outer enclosure in front of the main gate of the castle.

bastion A fortified stone wall.

battlements A low structure built on a wall for defence or decoration.

breach To break through.

Bronze Age The period of history that in ancient Greece lasted from 2000 to 1000 BCE.

casemate wall A fortified wall on which guns were often placed.

Celtic Relating to the Celts, a group of peoples who lived in much of Europe during the IRON AGE.

château A manor house, especially in France.

cistern A tank for storing water, sometimes underground.

citadel A stronghold inside or close to a city, or any strongly fortified building or refuge.

corbel A stone or timber jutting out from a wall to support the end of a beam or a platform.

crenellations Stone BATTLEMENTS jutting out of the castle walls.

curtain wall The wall that enclosed a castle courtyard.

donjon The medieval word for the KEEP of a castle.

embrasure An opening in a wall or PARAPET.

forebuilding A building that protected the entrance to a castle.

fresco A painting done in watercolours on wet plaster.

garrison The place where troops are stationed to guard a fortified building.

gilded Covered in gold, or a substance looking like gold.

grotto An artificial structure built to look like a natural cave.

hoarding A timber gallery built at the top of a wall or tower.

Iron Age The traditional name given to a time when smelting and the use of iron was widespread. It followed the BRONZE AGE.

keep The main tower of a castle – often able to defend itself without outside help.

lintel The flat top of a door or window.

loophole A slit or cross-shaped opening in

a castle wall through which archers fired their arrows.

machicolation An overhanging PARAPET or fighting gallery through which missiles could be dropped.

mason A person skilled in working in and building with stone.

moat A deep ditch around a castle, usually filled with water.

mortar (1) A cannon with a short barrel. (2) A mixture of lime with sand, cement and water used in building to join stones.

mosaic A design or decoration made of small pieces of glass, pottery or stone.

mosque A Muslim place of worship.

motte and bailey A castle in which the KEEP stands on top of a large mound of earth, called the motte, and is surrounded by a BAILEY.

parapet A wall to protect a castle and its soldiers.

parchment The treated skin of an animal used for writing on.

pavilion An open, ornamental building or decorative shelter.

petition A formal request to an authority, such as the king or emperor.

portcullis A grille, which slides up and down in grooves cut in the stones of a gateway.

postern A rear gate.

privy A small lavatory.

rampart The embankment surrounding a fort, including any walls built for defence.

refectory A dining hall.

rock-cut A tomb or cave carved from solid rock.

sally port A hidden entrance from which defenders could mount a surprise attack on invaders.

Saxon Relating to a people who lived in northern Germany and came to Britain from the 5th century CE.

scroll A roll of PARCHMENT used for writing on.

siege An operation carried out to capture a fortified place by surrounding it and not allowing people in or out.

synagogue A Jewish place of worship.

turret A small tower.

undermine To tunnel or dig under a building so it gradually becomes weaker.

vault An underground passage or room, often used for storage.

wattle and daub A way of making walls from woven twigs plastered with a mixture of clay, wood and sometimes chopped straw.

wickerwork Items such as baskets and fences made from twigs, usually willow, that are woven together.

Index